God and Evil:
An Ode to Kindness

Dwayne Cole

Parson's Porch Books
www.parsonsporchbooks.com

God and Evil: An Ode to Kindness
ISBN: Softcover 978-1-949888-64-5
Copyright © 2019 by Dwayne Cole

All rights reserved. No part of this book may be reproduced or transmitted in any form or by any means, electronic or mechanical, including photocopying, recording, or by any information storage and retrieval system, without permission in writing from the publisher.

*Evil is not so much a puzzle to be solved
as it is a mystery in which we live.*

Contents

Preface 7
Introduction 11
    Living with Unanswered Questions 11
Chapter One 22
    Evil in God's Good Creation 22
Chapter Two 34
    Jesus Gives a New Understanding of God and Evil ... 34
Chapter Three 40
    Evil and the God of Love in Jesus' Teachings 40
Chapter Four 50
    Understanding the Demonic in Jesus' Teachings 50
Chapter Five 55
    Our Continuing Struggle with Evil 55
Chapter Six 60
    Christian Guidelines for Coping with Evil 60
Chapter Seven 72
    A New Kindness 72
Chapter Eight 76
    A Relational Hermeneutic of Kindness for Interpreting the Bible's Story 76
Conclusion 93
Bibliography 97

Preface

Understanding evil and learning how to cope with it without being broken in the process is one of our greatest needs. This may also be our most difficult task, for we are dealing with the evolution of human consciousness and the nature of the complex human psyche, or soul. Carl G. Jung recognized the need for more study of the psyche, and he said often that humans are the origin of all coming evil.

Our tendency is to avoid the evil in our own lives like egotism, mental laziness, love of money, cowardice, prejudice, etc., and point to these same evils in others. When this happens, our neighbor becomes our enemy to be feared and walled out. Our fear compels us to have bigger guns and more powerful bombs for our protection. Persons and societies driven by fear are on the road to self-destruction.

Focusing on the psyche, i.e. the personal aspect of evil, is not enough, however. We experience evil as an impersonal force, often described as the demonic and as the cumulative evil acts of humans in society. Since we are born into a family, a society, and a world that we did not create, we can accurately describe evil as the evil we encounter in impersonal ways. For this reason, the demonic nature of evil will be a part of this study.

The main song of this book is that loving-kindness overcomes evil, and this truth must be born anew in our human psyche for us to gain a vision of hope. Our vision of hope affirms the reality of God and evil and examines both subjects from a hermeneutic of relational kindness, wherein each aspect of God expressed in trinitarian ways enriches the other. In these relational ways, God meets each occasion of our lives, including our struggle with evil, with kindness. Jesus modeled kindness, as did many prophets before him, and revealed its healing nature. God's Spirit empowers us for kindness, and as we learn to sing the "Ode to Kindness" we participate in transformation and healing.

Ode to Kindness

Kindness, Heart of God,
in your gentle care we enter.

All people become one
when your kindness is embraced.

God waits, the world waits,
longing for this new family.

Let us all taste the gift of tenderness,
the fruit of God's own self.

The kiss of kindness, a healing balm,
for all the world to share.

I wrote this Ode to Kindness after struggling with evil for fifty years as a Christian minister. Throughout my ministry evil was like the bass notes of life's daily experience. Some days I had the feeling that God who makes each beautiful day and meets it with kindness, also

breaks the rules and

takes life at will—

babies who die in the womb,

children who drown in swollen streams,

youth by the enemy's bomb,

adults with broken dreams.

Some days it is as though God walks

through the flower stalks,

and talks—don't do this

and don't do that whacking

with a switch the

flowers in their prime

Leaving us to pick up

the bleeding hearts.

I have a bleeding-heart flower bush by my condo. Each spring and summer its red flowers, each shaped like a bleeding heart, remind me of the fields of broken hearts I encountered in my ministry and still see around me.

Bleeding hearts so many

Pain so deep, so beyond reach

Only love can heal them.

With a prayer of love for healing, I dedicate this book to all of you who are being healed and who need to be healed from broken hearts, and with deep gratitude for those who have helped me in my times of brokenness to become a wounded healer. Special appreciation is given to Wayne Ozment who read this manuscript and offered helpful suggestions for clarity of its message. Also, deep gratitude goes to Beth, my wife. We met in a Greek class at seminary 55 years ago and have been married for 54 years. As a writer, editor, and manager of editors she has been a faithful listener and contributor to many of my thoughts expressed in this book.

Introduction

Living with Unanswered Questions

Evil is not a puzzle to be solved; it is a mystery in which we live.

Wendell was my best friend from the time we entered the first grade in school. We did all the things boys typically did growing up in the rural South in the post-depression decades of the forties and fifties. On the school grounds we played marbles and the daring game of follow the leader, which took us on adventures through the surrounding woods. In high school we played baseball and football. Wendell was a big guard in football, and he was good enough to consider a college and pro career. I was a lean and mean right end playing on both the offensive and defensive teams and lucky to be injury free after four years of tackling and being tackled. After canning his opposing guard, Wendell would make sure my lane stayed open on short pass plays. In fact, he could be one of the reasons I survived largely unscathed.

Then it happened. Just two weeks before graduation, Wendell was killed when two cars collided head-on at a curve in the road. His older brother, who was driving drunk was injured, but fully recovered, at least physically. The two elderly people in the other car, who were outstanding citizens and active church members were both also killed instantly. When I learned of the accident, I was stunned and filled with grief.

I remember going home from the funeral and climbing on the old Allis Chalmers farm tractor to cultivate the fields. I wanted to be alone with my troubling thoughts undisturbed. Soon a thunderstorm began to form, and the sky darkened, as though nature was in sympathy with my dark mood. Lightning flashed and thunder rolled. I cried out in the spirit of Job, shaking my fist at the heavens,

Why, O God,

did Wendell die

in this terrible car collision?

Why do you make

and then break

such a strong youth?

Did you really need another flower in heaven,

as the preacher said?

No answer came. The clouds were not rolled back, and there was no voice from heaven. But the storm passed on. The gentle rain came and washed away my tears. As the tractor rumbled on, I had a deep feeling of God's presence. A sparkling rainbow appeared on the horizon, and I found strength and hope in the glow of the rainbow to go on with my life.

Feeling somewhat better I took the tractor back to the shed to get some dry clothes. As I switched off the engine, I heard a whining noise. At first, I thought it was just the ringing of the tractor motor still reverberating through my eardrums

and up and down the corridors of my soul, but there it was again.

A soft whining

and a few little yelps could be heard

from the far corner of the shed.

As I approached the sounds,

I realized that it was my beagle,

another of my best friends;

and she was giving birth to four little pups.

Trembling, I watched in awe. Finally,

wanting to take part in this

miracle,

I picked one up and

held it close to my heart.

It too was trembling

and still frightened by birth.

I gently stroked the new born pup

held it like a cup

sipping a gentle kiss until it was calm.

Stroking with sweet balm.

Mother looked on with caressing eyes

and tender concern.

In the midst of the tragedy of death, I was witnessing new birth and new beginnings. This episode would always have meaning for me, and its impact would grow through the years.

For the person of faith,

all endings hold the possibilities of

new beginnings,

for God meets each occasion of our life

with kindness.

The shaking of our foundations

sometimes leads us to build new, stronger

foundations and thereon to erect greater

edifices.

At the funeral service for Wendell, the minister said this tragedy was God's will:

"We may not understand,

but we must not question.

We can only accept this as God's will."

Without knowing why at the time, this proclamation disturbed me.

As a farm boy with my fingers and toes planted in the soil,

I was much more at peace with growing crops,

The storm, the rain, the rainbow of

promise and security and hope, and

the birth of little beagle puppies,

these bathed my soul with

healing balm, comfort,

peace, and hope.

The idea of God taking the life of an eighteen-year-old youth in a cruel car accident was strange to my way of thinking. It did not resonate with my soul, but I simply did not have the words to express my feelings. Later my linguistic studies would reveal there are non-verbal and pre-reflective emotions, feelings, and thoughts that are virtually impossible to express in a one-to-one correlation to words and phrases. This recognition accounts for the movement from prose to poetry in this book and explains the sub-title, An Ode to Kindness.

In my studies and experience I have learned faith is best defined as something other than a system of beliefs or tenets. I found that doctrines and creeds written by persons of another age did not correspond with my inner feelings and emotions. For me faith is the acknowledgement and embodiment of these feelings or moods of existence through which God is revealed as a relational God who is always with us. However, only as I studied the gentle life and tender teachings of sages like Buddha, the Jewish prophets, Jesus, Martin Luther King,

Jr., and Mother Teresa did I experience a sense of inner resonance and harmony. Through the prism of kindness these feelings and moods became my personal and private beliefs through which the presence of God and God's loving care were revealed.

A lack of harmony can be unsettling for the individual believer as well as for the confessing community. This lack became real for me when I was ordained to Christian ministry. My ordination council, which included the oldest of my six brothers, asked me pointed questions from a book on doctrines and beliefs.

At that time, I was in college as a music and religion major, so let me use an analogy from music to explain. The tuning fork elicits a response from the piano, but only if the piano has a string tuned to the same frequency. The members on the ordination council were like the piano sounding out notes from the book of

doctrines. However, unlike the piano, I was not tuned to the same frequency.

To be sure, I grew up hearing many of these doctrines being preached every week

- that God is all-knowing and all-powerful
and controls every detail in the world (even cruel accidents);
- that God is lawgiver and judge who keeps a record of our deeds that determine whether one goes to heaven or hell;
- that God is unchanging and absolute.

In college I read in the fields of science, psychology, and philosophy. I began questioning some of these doctrinal concepts and wrestling, among other topics, with the classic problem of evil in our Christian experience: How can one explain the awful presence of evil in a good world created by an all-powerful and all-loving God? Some have put it this way,

> If God is all-powerful,
>
> God is able to rid the world of evil.

If God is all-loving,

God must want to rid the world of evil.

Since evil is a very real presence in the world,

God must not be both all-powerful and all-loving.

I had not found a solution to this classic problem of evil; I just felt deeply that the cruel car accident that took my friend's life was not God's will. I could not reconcile the ugly and evil death of my friend with the beauty and goodness of God's creation that I had experienced in my large and loving family on the farm. Also, I could not reconcile the angry feelings I felt in my grief with the love of God I knew through my parents and at times through my church family. A loving and good God just could not have taken Wendell's life in a cruel accident.

While I have not solved the problem of evil, I have learned as a pastor for fifty years that evil is not so much a puzzle to be solved as it is a mystery

in which we live.

I have learned that it is okay

to ask questions like these—

Who is responsible for evil?

Why does evil exist in God's good world?

Where does evil come from?

Does God give and then take life?

As a minister I have had to face my own evil and my own questions as well as the questions of thousands of church members. My concern was always to first offer a shoulder to cry on and compassion for broken and bleeding hearts. Theological answers would come later in small group sessions organized around these concerns. Instead, I sought to offer practical help in coping with evil in order to keep evil from breaking them in the process.

Nurture and inner shaping, what psychologists call **efficient causation** and **self-actualization**, are well established principles of growth and development. After studying about them I now recognize I have been nurtured (efficient causation) and shaped by the persuasive love of family and God (self-actualization, since this has been an inner shaping by persuasion instead of coercive power). As a result, my inner feelings and emotions do not resonate with the stale doctrines about God's omnipotent and unchanging nature.

This understanding does not mean I do not respect my tradition and my ordination council. One does not throw away the cradle of one's faith even if one is outgrowing its clothing. Also, it does not mean I think doctrines are unnecessary. It does mean our theological beliefs must always be growing and changing to correspond to the Spirit's moving and our inner feelings.

>The Spirit comes
>
>like a gentle wind
>
>that ruffles the curtains
>
>at dawn,
>
>or wafts like the sweet perfume
>
>of wildflowers in the meadow,
>
>bringing change and new ways of seeing things.

Most Protestants claim to be "Christo-centric," i.e. their doctrines and creeds are Christ-centered. Yet, the most original element in Jesus' life, his total **God- consciousness,** will forever remain un-formalized. This total dedication to God's will lay within Jesus' **pre-**

reflective consciousness and experience. Jesus alluded to this experience in his statement in John 10:30——*the Father and I are one.* Jesus lived and died secure in this conviction.

As Christians we follow one who voluntarily gave his life, and this is of primary importance. Doctrines about Jesus are secondary in importance to his life as told in the Gospels. Thus,

> the gentle life and tender teachings of Jesus
>
> are the touchstone of our faith
>
> and will help us understand evil.

We need ever and again to return to Jesus' life and teachings. The vivid records of the eyewitnesses to Jesus contained in the New Testament Gospels are crucial. These writers recorded the life and teachings of Jesus while at the same time were the first responders to it. And this is the complicating factor. Separating the evangelists' words as Gospel writers from the authentic words of Jesus is hard. However, New Testament scholars can agree Jesus was gentle and his teachings were kind.

When the gentle life and tender teachings of Jesus flow as a freshet, a stream of fresh water, through all of the church's doctrines and creeds, they will be refreshed and give new life to our beliefs. Then our lives become one with Jesus and God, resonating as one with our doctrines, like tuning fork and piano tuned to the same frequency.

To be sure, the first eyewitnesses responded to the life and teachings of Jesus in different ways, as can be seen in an analysis of the four Gospels, Matthew, Mark, Luke, and John. As critical study of the Gospels has taught us, especially redaction criticism, each Gospel has its own distinctive theology.

Each writer had the freedom to shape the faith stories circulating in the communities to meet the needs of each particular community and the problems encountered there. The writer of the Gospel of John showed the most creative freedom to shape and re-shape the early Jesus traditions. The Gospel writers show us the Jesus tradition is not formalized creeds but is a living tradition, alive with spiritual, transformative power. Those today who want to make the Scriptures literal and fixed fail to see the creative freedom of those who wrote these books. The church needs to always be free to refresh its doctrines when they become stale, stumbling blocks to unity and cooperative ministries in combating the world's evil in Jesus' name. The church should also be flexible enough to allow for differing expressions of faith and doctrine in different religious bodies.

God, as **creative-responsive-kindness,**

is confronting the world with unrealized aims

and novel possibilities at all times.

This flexibility implies the church's need for experiencing *creative transformation of the past* by sharing in God's responsive kindness and its being open to the future. The literalist's theology, whether fundamentalist or conservative, will ultimately fail if this necessity for creative transformation is not realized and even encouraged. That's true because rigidity fights against the essence of an ever-changing, evolving universe.

The next chapter will anchor evil in the creative process and attempt to understand God as creative-responsive-kindness rather than as coercive power. While this approach will still not solve the puzzle of evil, the mystery will be more manageable, and we will gain a more worthy view of God that can inspire our lives and our worship.

There seems to be no limit to books on evil. At the age of ten my grandson pointed to my bookshelf and about two dozen books there with evil in the title and asked, "Granddaddy, why do you have so many books on evil?" (Interested readers will find many of these sources listed in the bibliography at the end of this book). I acknowledge appreciation for all who have written on the relationship of God and evil. However, I will not burden the reader with excessive footnotes to these writers. My material has been filtered through my study in college and seminary with three graduate level degrees and 50 years of pastoral experience.

Chapter One

Evil in God's Good Creation

"In the beginning God created the heavens and the earth. The earth was barren, with no form or life" (Genesis 1:1-2a).

God looked at all that had been called out of chaos and "All of it was very good" (Genesis 1:31, authors paraphrase).

Adam and Eve

Over eons of evolutionary time,

desiring a beautiful garden

in which to stroll,

God said, "I will call forth

green trees and plants.

Add some flowers and bees."

God walked in the garden

and was pleased.

Still wanting to share more goodness,

seeking to add to

the buzz of the bees,

God called forth Adam and Eve.

Walking in the garden with kin, dressed only

in their shiny new skin God was very pleased.

The snake looked on

With a sly grin!

For many religions, including Christianity, these **poetic-mythic** verses from Genesis, Chapter 1, present the starting point for all thoughts about God, the world, and all things in the world. **Our understanding of both good and evil is grounded in these beginnings and rooted in the evolving human consciousness.**

In these mythic accounts, God, as the source of all creative possibilities, is mysteriously prior to all things that have evolved from chaotic beginnings. God, as the source of heavenly possibilities, provides the eternal, unifying value of all that is called into being, including all life forms.

> Using mystifying language, the biblical writers show how
>
> God meets each evolving entity
>
> with goodness and kindness,
>
> feeling and receiving all that is coming into being,
>
> into God's own unifying being
>
> and redeeming purpose,
>
> showing a tender patience
>
> that loses nothing that can be saved.

The world is saved and shaped toward goodness, kindness, and love as it is drawn by way of the gentle life and tender teachings of the prophets and Jesus into the immediacy of God's own life of loving-kindness.

The writers of Genesis interpreted God's goodness through their own mythic world view, using poetic language similar to that of the Babylonian creation myths. Interpreting this inspiring vision for our lives today deserves the best insights of philosophy, psychology, theology, biblical faith, and science, all of which have shaped our world view.

These insights about God and the world were shaped by reading Alfred North Whitehead, the father of process philosophy, and those in this school of thought like Charles Hartshorne, John B. Cobb, Jr., David Ray Griffin, Lewis S. Ford, and Marjorie Hewitt Suchocki. Marjorie Suchocki's books, such as *God Christ Church: A Practical Guide to Process Theology,* have also shaped my thought. Marjorie's words and phrases have a way of sticking in one's vocabulary and thought patterns and for that I am grateful.

Since the writers of Genesis used the **poetic-mythic** world view of their day to express their faith in God, they present us a living account, not a set belief system for all ages. For by its nature, poetic myth speaks in ever fresh and new ways. Faith is a relationship with a creative luring God who is in the evolving process and in our lives with loving aims and redeeming purposes, helping us to become our very best selves.

God and Chaos

With God's vision of goodness and loving-kindness daily transforming our lives, then why is there so much chaotic evil in our lives and in God's good world? Where does evil come from? (For an excellent source that deals with the origin of Satan in the Hebrew and Christian Scriptures, see Elaine Pagels, *The Origin of Satan).*

I am reluctant to say evil is a part of the chaos out of which creation arose. To say this would suggest dualism, the existence of a powerful force apart from God. Yet, paradoxically

> evil emerges out of the evolving human consciousness
>
> for it is our consciousness that names good and evil and
>
> makes value judgments concerning good and evil.

In what sense is the presence of good and evil in the world and in our lives paradoxical?

A paradox is a truth

too big for simple answers.

In an attempt to solve the paradox of good and evil, Carl Jung conceived a shadow, a dark side of God incarnated in the world. This dark thought led Jung to write, "Answer to Job," a treatise that reveals polarities, tensions between ideas, in Jung's thought. Jung, like Jesus and the apostle Paul in the New Testament saw evil within human nature, in the shadow side of human nature. Thus, evil is the outcome of our conscious human nature and our freedom to choose a way apart from God. Paradoxically, evil for

Jung is located in the heart of God *and* in the heart of human beings.

In Job we see

God and Satan Sparring---

Let's put our boxing gloves on

and enter the ring,

spar a little with God and Satan

as Job's tag partner.

Satan enters the ring first.

Lifts his fist in the air

like Ali, the heavyweight champ.

Like a great agitator

Satan brings Job into the ring

and paints him as God's golden boy,

God's pet if you will.

Ah, God, can't you see that Job worships you

because you have greatly blessed him with

family, health, and great wealth.

Take away these and watch him fall to the canvas defeated,

cursing you and the day he was born.

The shadow boxing between God and Satan

becomes reality for Job.

God agrees and lets Satan strip Job down to bare bones,

taking away his sons and daughters in a whirlwind,

removing his herds,

and inflicting Job himself with a sickness near death.

Three of Job's friends put on their gloves and

enter the ring with

their crystal-cathedral gospel of wealth as a sign of blessings.

They believe Job's loss is

a clear sign of God's punishment of Job for his sins.

Job with boxing gloves lifted before his face

murmurs, I am innocent.

Job and his friends spar back and forth

the contest ending in a draw.

The three friends remove their gloves and go home.

Beaten and bruised, Job wonders if humans

can ever find God's wisdom,

God's answers to the mystery of suffering.

Lying prostrate on the mat,

he continues to say, I am innocent!

I have done no wrong!

Pounding the dirt-floor mat

Job says,

I have never mistreated the land

and made it mourn.

I grew wheat standing tall and waving in the gentle breeze,

not weeds and thorns that inflict pain.

With this tender note sounded

Job's real friend comes in and takes his hand.

Stand up Job we will fight this battle together!

We were made from clay

and often do not understand God's ways.

As he spars several rounds with God and Satan,

Job's friend wavers from the blows,

not quite sure from where the punch of illness comes.

Maybe it is punishment for sins.

There are some days when the storms come

like a fist punching from the dark sky.

Lightning strikes and thunder roars.

We cover our face with our gloves

and seek refuge on the ropes

maybe sitting cowered in the corner of the ring.

Then the sun breaks out like a bright angel of hope,

offering new possibilities for victory.

The glorious splendor of God

is greater than the warm glow of sun

after dark clouds have dispersed.

In this heavenly light,

the fist that pounds in the storms,

opens,

revealing kindness,

healing our wrongs.

God is infinitely fair, patient, forgiving.

Continuing his poem

praising God's care of nature,

Job's true friend invites him to a banquet table,

saying the rainstorms are necessary

to provide your favorite foods.

Come feast on the many wonders of God.

Receive the undeserved grace of God.

In the context of grace and feasting

God who cares for nature appears.

God is introduced as one who

laid the foundation for the earth

and set the stars in place.

God affirms Jobs faithfulness

and blesses him

by making him

twice as wealthy as he was

before this sparring match began.

Job never understood his suffering

but he sings a victory song---

I know that my redeemer lives

One day I will see God;

by this faith I will forever live.

(See Job 33, 36, 37, in the *Contemporary English Version* of the Bible for the theme of kindness).

The apostle Paul in Romans 1:18-32 wrote of the wrath of God in terms similar to the shadow side of God as found in Carl Jung. In my research for a paper I wrote in seminary on the wrath of God, I learned this passage is the only place in the Bible where the wrath of God is discussed in detail. A close study of this passage convinced me that

wrath is affective

    and not effective;

        it is a feeling

            and not an action.

The wrath of God is the feeling of God when humans commit evil acts and self-destruct as a result of their choice.

The wrath of God is not thunderbolts and lightning flashing.

    It is humans closing their eyes to the light of God,

        their ears to the saving words of God,

            and their heart to God's relational love.

Humans judged they would be better off not being in a loving relationship with God. So God allowed them to choose their own evil way. Primary throughout this discussion in Romans is this declaration: God gives God's self to persons but never forces or coerces. Humans have the freedom to choose their own way.

The biblical message is about God cultivating a special relationship of love with the people of God.

> God is in the world
>
> and for the world,
>
> feeling our pain and sorrow.
>
> God meets each occasion of life
>
> with kindness,
>
> and lures humans toward the fulfillment
>
> of kindness in their lives.

So, perhaps, God having the feeling of wrath is not surprising when God's loving-kindness is spurned. In covenant with God this truth is central:

God's feeling is always clothed in a covenant of faithful love.

> God's relational love is persuasive and luring
>
> not coercive and controlling.

Humans have *evolved with* freedom to choose. When humans fail to be transformed by God's loving aims and saving purposes, their failure is sin. Sin in the Bible may be defined as the failure to achieve the good that God intends for us. The most common word for sin in the Greek New Testament is *hamartia and* is best translated as "missing the mark of God's intention for our lives." In the Genesis story, Adam and Eve had the capacity to choose good; but they chose evil and missed God's aim and purpose for them. This capacity to choose good is a part of the evolutionary process. Thus, there is a correlation between the possibility for good and the possibility for evil.

We find a resolution to this dilemma of God and evil in the Gospels of the New Testament and the example of Jesus. The most original element in Jesus' life was his total **God-consciousness**. This total dedication to God's will lay within Jesus' **pre-reflective consciousness** and experience. Jesus' gentle life and tender teachings are the culmination of a thousand years of covenant in which God nurtured a special relationship with Israel. This culmination is the meaning of the New Testament phrase, "Jesus came in the fullness of time." In fulfilling God's loving aims and redeeming purposes, Jesus became a model for all humanity. Jesus lived and died in the secure faith that

the Father and I are one (John 14:10).

The next chapter will seek to show how Jesus' gentle life and tender teachings gave a new understanding of God and evil, especially how we can best cope with evil.

Chapter Two

Jesus Gives a New Understanding of God and Evil

The gentle life and tender teachings of Jesus give us, as Christians, the clearest understanding we have of God and evil; and they are, therefore, the touchstone of our faith. We must ever and again return to this gentle life and these tender teachings. The vivid records of the eyewitnesses to Jesus' life contained in the New Testament Gospels are crucial for our understanding of Jesus. These writers saw and documented the life of Jesus while also being the first to respond to his tender love. In Jesus' life and teachings **tender love energies** appeared that slowly transform our lives and our world.

This gentle life

evokes the best in human nature:

The gentle mother,

the baby Jesus,

the lowly servant teacher.

The message of kindness and love

all without force or coercion

yet with the authority

of heaven's stamp of approval.

Galilean images

dreams of an unrealized world

Jesus like a mirror

in which we look

to see the face of God;

Jesus preached the Gospel

not only in word,

but also in images

of birds and flowers,

crops and fields.

Jesus' gentle life spoke

and his kind words acted.

Ordinary words with

extraordinary meaning.

Each spoken word,

Each acted word,

wrapped in a miracle

of healing kindness.

I find this understanding of Jesus reveals God's power as persuasive kindness. Of his miracles, Jesus' feeding of the five thousand is the only one recorded in all four Gospels. Some people who heard and were fed by Jesus that day waned to force the coming of God's kingdom which is best understood as God's rule in the lives of people. After the miracle, they were about to seize

Jesus and make him king by force. John said,

> Jesus went off again to the hills
>
> by himself to pray (John 6:15).

The first three Gospels—Matthew, Mark, and Luke—tell us that Jesus struggled with the kind of Messiah he would be at the beginning of his ministry. In these three wilderness temptations Jesus faced a critical decision:

Would he be—

1. A popular Messiah (temptation to turn stones into bread and feed the hungry).

2. A spectacular Messiah (temptation to leap from the Temple spire).

3. A political Messiah (temptation to become king).

Jesus rejected all three temptations, refusing to turn from the role of suffering servant. The third temptation, to become a military messiah, may have been the most appealing and difficult for him. This role was what most contemporary Jews expected of the Messiah. Why not ride on a great white horse and have the world bow down at your feet? Jesus declined, however, choosing a better way. He knew what some judges and prophets of the Old Testament who thought God commissioned warfare and violent destruction didn't know; and what the dictators of this world who worship at the feet of power and coercion still don't know: the kingdom of God could not be formed by such methods. In fact, the kingdom of this world and all earthly power must be transformed by the royal loving-kindness of God to be just and civil.

As one who had chosen the way of lowly service and not the way of worldly power; Jesus would not climb to the "pinnacle of the temple" (Matthew 4:6, NSRV) to perform a spectacular leap of faith. Instead,

> he would climb Calvary's hill
>
> to dash his life against an old
>
> rugged cross.

The crowd always wants a God of powerful and spectacular actions, but Jesus understood that sacrificial love would be the real drawing power:

> "When I am lifted up from the earth,
>
> I will draw everyone to me (John 12:32).

The wisdom of the ages has proven Jesus right. People are not won by sham and show, but by sacrificial love and kindness.

> The world needs not a sign,
>
> but a Savior!

Jesus' gentle Galilean ministry that operated by love and healing kindness is what gives meaning to the way he died. Two thieves died alongside Jesus, one on his right and one on his left. They were crucified, but we don't call them Savior! The cross of Jesus would lose most of its meaning without the gentle Galilean ministry that preceded it. At the same time his teachings would have less meaning if he had not been willing to die for them. There is a unity to the teachings and the death of Jesus. His words acted kindness and his actions spoke kindness!

Jesus summed up all of his teachings in one great commandment of lovingkindness: Love the Lord your God with all your heart, with all your soul, with all your mind, and with all your strength. . ... Love your neighbor as you love yourself (Mark 12:29-30). Jesus lived and died for this message of love. The First Epistle of John says,

> "This is how we know what love is:
>
> Christ gave his life for us" (1 John 3:16).

An event just prior to his crucifixion also shows that Jesus chose persuasive love over coercive force. When the Roman soldiers and temple police came to arrest Jesus in the garden, Peter drew a sword and cut off a man's ear. Jesus rebuked Peter and told him to put up his sword (John 18:10-11), saying

> He would drink the cup of suffering.
>
> He would voluntarily lay down his life on the cross
>
> as an expression of love for all persons.

The church has skipped over the gentle life and tender teachings of Jesus for the power of the sword and has the traits of Caesar instead of those of God. We are forever creating God in our own image. But Jesus' life, teachings, and death all show God to be a God of persuasive love, not coercive power.

Christian theology is simply words about God. This chapter has shown that Jesus is the clearest Word we have about God. God relates to the world and to us with creative-responsive love.

The next chapter will seek to show that Jesus' gentle life and tender teachings are the best prism we have for understanding both God and evil.

Chapter Three

Evil and the God of Love in Jesus' Teachings

Christian theologians have sought the source of evil and how to cope with it from the time Jesus gave his gentle teachings two thousand years ago. The Gospel of Mark (the first of the Gospels to have been written and used as a primary source for Matthew and Luke), places great emphasis on Jesus' confrontation with evil and his healing of those broken by evil. In Mark evil is the foe of Jesus as Messiah and is named as Satan and demons. In this chapter we will demonstrate this conflict and healing by examining Mark 1:21-28, an incident that occurred in the synagogue in Capernaum.

Jesus called his disciples to share in his ministry of defeating evil. I once thought the primary message of these stories was for the church to share in this ministry. I would read the stories of healing and feel compelled to become a compassionate, caring, healing minister.

However, I have increasingly realized the church has skipped over the first purpose of these healing stories saturated with evil.

You and I must first see ourselves as the fragmented,

broken person crying out to Jesus for healing.

We must first see ourselves

as the wounded person by the Jericho roadside

in need of the good Samaritan to bind up our wounds.

Evil is imbedded in our hearts but believing in the Good News of God's saving love brings healing to our lives. Only when the church is healed can it become the wounded-healer.

In Jesus' day the roadways were littered with broken individuals, even as our city streets are today. Illnesses, both physical and mental, were attributed to demons. Demon possession was seen as a common experience in the time of Jesus, and the gentle teachings of Jesus are filled with the healing of persons possessed by demons. The Gospel of Mark records several grizzly accounts of exorcisms Jesus performed. On one occasion, Jesus was in the synagogue at Capernaum teaching when a man with an evil spirit came in and screamed,

'What do you want with us,

Jesus of Nazareth?

Are you here to destroy us?

I know who you are—

You are God's holy messenger!'

Jesus ordered the spirit,

'Be quiet and come out of the man!'

The evil spirit shook the man hard,

gave a loud scream and came out of him (Mark 1:21-25).

Mark 1:27 reports that the people who witnessed this act of Jesus were amazed. I am amazed just reading about it!

Where is the Word of God in these healing stories for us today? We'll get to that topic later in this chapter. For now, this much is clear: demon exorcisms and healing miracles were integral to the mission and message of Jesus, and they are central to the Gospels' stories in the New Testament. Jesus' tender words teach, heal, and exorcise demons. The exorcisms were action sermons that demonstrated the compassion of God and proclaimed the coming of the kingdom of God. In the Lord's Prayer Jesus interprets the kingdom of God as a time when God's will is done on earth as it is in heaven. In bringing God near, Jesus brought the rule or kingdom of God near. Jesus' first recorded message was:

> The kingdom of God is at
>
> hand, repent
>
> and believe
>
> the gospel (Mark 1:15).

Why Did Jesus Perform Miracles?

According to the Synoptic Gospels (Matthew, Mark, and Luke), as soon as Jesus announced the coming of God's kingdom, he went out to meet the power of evil head on. This sequencing has led some to think Jesus performed these miracles of exorcisms to prove his divinity—to show his power was greater than the demons. I would rather think that

> Jesus performed miracles
>
> to share his **love energies.**
>
> Love's power lies in
>
> the desire to enrich others.

God's love in Jesus is responsive love. Jesus could not walk through Galilee as God's messenger without responding to the broken persons he encountered. His loving touch energized these helpless individuals and gave them new hope and new life. Stephen Spielberg's *E. T.* was not the first to touch with the finger and give energy and new life.

Many of Jesus' miracles can be interpreted as miracles of compassion. Ten times the Synoptic Gospels present Jesus as one with divine compassion. Using the Greek terms, σπλαγχνον and σπλαγχνιζομαι, as in Mark 1:41, is the strongest way possible to stress the tender compassion of Jesus. We get the expressions "heart-felt" and "gut feeling" from this word. It speaks of a deep, inner pity or compassion for another person.

After announcing the kingdom of God was near, Jesus began to perform miracles of heart-felt compassion. (See, for example, Mark 1:41, Luke 7:13, and Matthew 20:34).

>Jesus had compassion on the man
>
>with a dreaded skin disease and healed him.
>
>Jesus had compassion on the widow of Nain
>
>and raised her dead son back to life.
>
>Jesus had compassion on the blind men
>
>and restored their sight.

True compassion implies the willingness to suffer with the needy.

In responsive love

>Jesus suffered

> with the leper
>
> the broken-hearted mother,
>
> and the blind men.

Jesus identified with those who were suffering. Their wounds were his wounds; their pains were his pains. Thus, the miracles of Jesus were acts of compassion that showed the kingdom of God coming near.

How Was Jesus Able to Perform Miracles?

We turn now from the why of Jesus' miracles to the how. How was Jesus able to perform such great miracles? The answer must surely be sought in the power of miraculous **love energies.**

> God who spoke
>
> and brought order
>
> out of disorder
>
> and cosmos out of chaos,
>
> spoke in Jesus to bring
>
> wholeness out of brokenness
>
> and life out of death.

Jesus was totally confident of God's presence in his life and ministry, and it was exemplified in the way he spoke to God as a child speaks to a parent. This confidence enabled him to act with authority and power.

So, how was Jesus able to cast this evil spirit out of this man in Capernaum described in Mark 1:21-28? Jesus taught that perfect love casts out fear (I John 4:18). This passage also applies to fear of demons. Jesus' powerful, Spirit-filled love words and love actions evoked new levels of energy and power in the broken persons he encountered. The fusion of these powerful **love energies** with the willing faith of the needy persons brought cleansing and wholeness.

You and I can understand the power of Jesus' loving touch in this man's life, because we know the end of the gospel story—we know the power of the cross and the resurrection. As the Gospel writers told these stories, they also knew the transforming power of these events. In fact, they wrote after the resurrection, and could then go back to the beginning, the birth with new understanding. Their communities had also experienced the creative and transforming power of the cross and the victory over evil on Easter morning. The cross and resurrection proved once and for all that the power of evil was broken!

With this knowledge and conviction of the victory of love over hate, the Gospel writers could faithfully report what Jesus said to the evil spirits possessing people's lives: "Be quiet and come out!" (Mark 1:25). These healing words were striking and astonishing acts! Not only because Jesus had the power to perform them; we know that from knowing the end of the story. In the demon exorcism in Mark 1, the man was astounded because

> Jesus cared enough
>
> to come close to him.

From the history of that era we know the man most likely was shunned by his own people. They thought he deserved his miserable, demon-possessed life because of his sin. Jesus disregarded this shunning tradition and accepted him as a child of God who needed a loving word of acceptance. The Greek word used to describe the man's life is σπαραξαν, which in classical Greek meant "to tear" or "rend," and here probably means "convulse." The poor man's life had been torn apart by the evil spirit, which then made one last convulsing gasp before obeying Jesus and coming out of the man. The demon could do nothing else for he himself knew what we also know—

that Jesus is the Holy One of God!

The crowd was also astonished and amazed.

They responded—What is this?

Is it some kind of new teaching?

The clue to understanding the crowd's amazement was not that Jesus could cast out the spirit. Magicians of that day could do the same. So why was the crowd amazed? Two words in the text give us the clue:

καινη, meaning "new,"

and ακαθάρτων, meaning "defiled" or "unclean."

Since the crowd saw the man as "unclean," they would stay far away from him. To touch him, even accidentally, would mean they were defiled. They would have to go through cleansing rituals to purify themselves. So, their traditional laws allowed them to shout,

"Stay away!"

Even the unclean man was supposed to shout this as he walked along.

Thus, what astonished them was that Jesus would come near to the man.

> It must be "a new teaching,'
>
> for the old said loud and clear—
>
> "Stay away!"

Now we are ready to answer the question, "What is the Word of God for us in this grizzly little story?" And by implication, in all the miracle stories of Jesus. Central to our Good News story is the cry,

> the Holy One of God is with us!

Our evil-riddled society is wondering if any divine reality is working for good in the world. Needy individuals are asking if any loving touch can bring healing to their lives. Our world is filled with the "torn ones"—the homeless fill our streets. Just as the synagogue crowd shunned this torn and convulsing man, churches today shun the poor and needy.

Jesus drew the demonic man into the pure and non-coercive love of God, and that love had the power to heal and bring wholeness out of brokenness. The crowd was amazed, and our world will be amazed when the church breaks down the barriers of race, gender, and poverty.

> When we love all people
>
> with the pure love of God,
>
> our world will once again
>
> be amazed and
>
> astounded!

People today live with many demonic fears. And fear is the antithesis of trusting love and the parent of hate and retaliation. The man in Mark's story was caught in the grip of this fear and cried out to Jesus, "Are you here to destroy us?" Notice the man referred to himself as "us." He was a man of multiple personalities—his demons were many. In a real sense Jesus was there to destroy the demons. They believed demons lurked along the path of life in rocks and trees.

Such fears controlled daily life then. That you and I can go a day without thinking of demons shows Jesus did destroy the demons.

He brought and lived the creative, transforming power of the kingdom of God. In his life,

> heavenly realities were shining
>
> in a dark, demon-infested world.

According to Mark 7:14-23, Jesus located evil in the human heart. This insight was and is new, fresh, and authoritative. And it is a discovery that makes evil manageable. As long as evil is located outside of us, we can escape responsibility, saying that the devil made me do it! Yet, it is our inner life that is divided and torn.

> Jesus knew the evil of the human
>
> heart and with love
>
> he sought to take possession
>
> of this heart
>
> for the kingdom of God.
>
> Love unites and heals

Evil is the dark background against which Jesus' gentle teachings shine all the brighter. So, the story in Mark, chapter one, closes with this happy refrain:

> The news about Jesus spread quickly.
>
> And why not?
>
> **Galilean glories** were shining
>
> with the light of kingdom of heaven realities,
>
> overcoming the dark, evil forces
>
> that plague people's lives.

Chapter Four

Understanding the Demonic in Jesus' Teachings

How do we understand the demonic in the teachings of Jesus? Some in theological circles understand demons in **ontological** terms, i.e., seeing them as real beings that are other than human. We will treat the term demonic as a dimension of the **shadow side of our human nature,** using Carl G. Jung's understanding of our human psyche As mentioned earlier, psychotherapist Jung revealed a balanced view of human nature that respects the biblical understanding and the fragmented human psyche. The biblical and psychological viewpoints are not incompatible and can be respected.

The gentle life and tender teachings of Jesus revealed in the New Testament give us a good perspective for understanding evil and the demonic. The first Epistle of John describes fear as the opposite of love and the basis of destructive demonic forces.

> Love as revealed in Jesus' gentle life and tender teachings overcomes and dispels fear.

Jesus, as we do, took seriously demonic power but he also showed us our role is to choose love over fear and demonic determinism. We must accept responsibility for evil!

No one understood the human psyche and our responsibility for evil better than Carl Jung. He personally saw the ugly side of society's behavior in the slaughter of six million Jews under the Nazis. Little wonder Jung believed that only when we see and understand the threats of powerful world leaders can we hope to cope with evil. For Jung this requires that we understand the duality of our nature and our individual capacity for good and evil. Jung wrote a brilliant and searching inquiry into this dilemma with the title, *The Undiscovered Self.*

Only as we recognize the **shadow side** within all of us can we have the humility and modesty required to deal with evil and good. Jung saw the need of a change-agent in coping with evil. I believe this change-agent can be seen best in the gentle life and tender teachings of Jesus who **self-actualized** the kindness God shows us in every occasion of our lives. This kindness is healing and transforming.

> The kindness we show to ourselves,
>
> our families, our community,
>
> and to our world
>
> is the most healing force in life
>
> we can experience.

The disciples caught this vision of kindness from Jesus and it would change their lives forever. It enabled them to harmonize their activities with Jesus' vision of the kingdom of God and propelled them on a transforming adventure. Yet

> this vision of gentle kindness has largely remained
>
> an unfulfilled dream.
>
> We need to recapture this
>
> dream and let it propel us
>
> forward and upward
>
> to new heights of creativity.

Why has Jesus' vision of transforming kindness not been fulfilled to a larger degree? Because as Jesus knew human nature is capable of infinite good and of infinite evil. In process theology terms, we might describe this as the human capacity for intrinsic good and intrinsic evil, a concept that is true to Jesus' teachings. As stated in the previous chapter, according to Mark 7:14-23, Jesus located evil in the human heart. Consider his words: Jesus called the crowd together "Pay attention and try to understand what I mean. The food that you put into your mouth doesn't make you unclean and unfit to worship God. The bad words that come out of your mouth are what make you unclean—What comes from your heart is what makes you unclean.

> Out of your heart comes evil thoughts,
>
> vulgar deeds, stealing,
>
> murder, unfaithfulness in marriage,
>
> greed,
>
> meanness,
>
> deceit,
>
> indecency,
>
> envy, insults, pride, and foolishness.
>
> All of these come from your heart,
>
> and they are what make you unfit to worship God.

In this teaching Jesus confronted the understanding of the demonic of his day. For Jesus evil does not come from a personal being outside of us,

but from our own human heart within us.

Using this understanding Jesus sought to capture the human psyche for the kingdom of God. In the Bible, heart and mind are synonyms, both referring to the center of one's being.

A corollary of the intrinsic nature of good and evil, locating both in the human psyche, is what we might call the instrumental nature of good and evil, i.e., the way we affect others as they deal with their dual nature of good and evil. Evil is like a contagious disease that seems to always be on the rebound, growing with each new occurrence.

To express this truth, I wrote this poem based on Jesus' parable of the return of an evil spirit that had been cast out of a man's life (Luke 11:24-26).

I shot the devil and he came back

bringing seven more from his demon pack.

Dropped bombs, blowing the hinges

from the doors of hell,

releasing a legion of demons

to walk to and fro on the earth

wreaking havoc.

This is the nature of vengeance—

It grows with each new occurrence.

And some say that the only way to

stop a bad man with a gun

is a good man with a gun!

Or build bigger bombs.

I shot the devil and he came back.

Bringing seven more from his demon pack.

In the following chapter, I will gather some of the truths already stated and, in summary fashion, weave them into an understanding of our personal struggle with evil. This next chapter will further reveal the reality of the rebounding nature of evil.

Chapter Five

Our Continuing Struggle with Evil

As mentioned in the introduction, I started exploring the subject of evil in college religion courses in 1960. I continued to seek a solution to my grief and the classic problem of evil in the seminary from 1964-73. Since then I have pursued this quest for over 50 years as a parish minister and adjunct college and seminary instructor. As a minister I had to deal with my evil nature and at the same time offer some help to those who experienced various forms of evil. These forms included the death of a child, a youth killed in the war in Viet Nam, a husband and father entangled in unethical business deals, and many tragic illnesses.

In my ministry I sought to reconcile the angry feelings my church members had on these tragic occasions. I still have not solved the problem of evil. In fact, I have learned that evil is not so much a puzzle to be solved as it is a mystery to be lived. How can one explain the awful presence of evil in a good world created by an all-powerful and all-loving God? Here is a restatement of the problem expressed thus far in preceding chapters and in many books on evil:

1. If God is all-powerful, God is able to rid the world of evil.

2. If God is all-loving, God must want to rid the world of evil.

3. Yet evil is a very real presence in the world.

4. Therefore, God must not be both all-powerful and all-loving.

So far, I have shown that how one experiences God determines how one responds to such reasoning. Many see God as a lawgiver and judge—a Cosmic Moralist who punishes people for wrongdoing, sometimes even with death. The relational theology I am developing has a richer, fuller view of God than this cold, abstract legalism.

The minister who conducted the funeral service for my friend understood God as Controlling Power—a God who determines every detail of life. Thus, if a loved one dies, one accepts it without asking questions, even cruel death in an automobile crash caused by someone driving drunk. I have found a different understanding of God's power. I see God operating in the world by persuasive-creative-responsive love rather than by coercive force.

The attributes that characterize God are goodness, kindness, and love. God is always good and loving. God promotes the greatest good for all at all times.

God is always in the world and for the world, feeling and relating to each event. Understanding God in this relational way implies change. This understanding is true because energy is not static, and the energy of God's love involves change and newness. For God as well as for humans, new events become knowable only in the moment that they happen. Thus, we can say this aspect of God's knowledge waits on, is dependent on, human decisions and worldly events.

God knew and continues to know the possibility of actions that are free, i.e. not predetermined. God has placed good and loving aims within the creative process. These aims become reality only when humans make decisions for goodness and love. Thus, the possibility for intrinsic goodness and the corresponding capacity for intrinsic evil always exists. Since humans have the freedom to embody both good and evil, they have the corresponding capacity to become instruments of both good and evil. Thus, evil becomes actual when humans decide for evil.

This understanding of God's nature has illuminated our understanding of the problem of evil in God's good creation.

However, we need to explore a step further how the Creator chooses to relate to creation.

When the minister at my friend's funeral spoke of God in terms of controlling power and coercive force, he was expressing the viewpoint of many Christians. According to this notion God determines and shapes every aspect of the world and life. Thus, when my friend was killed in the car accident, the minister could only say, "God took our loved one." For him, God controls every detail of life. Many who follow this way of thinking would say Wendell was delivered from this vale of suffering and is enjoying a fuller life with God forever.

Some theologians go a step further and add that this life is a vale of suffering that prepares us for our fuller life with God. To them, the purpose of life with all its suffering is "soul making" (See John Hicks, *Evil and the God of Love*, for this idea of "soul making).

The biblical revelation shaping the relational theology in this book offers a different interpretation. The question of whether God is able to shape all things is the wrong starting point. In terms of God's eternal nature, God is omnipotent. However, in terms of the way God feels about all of creation, God relates to the world in a responsive, persuasive way, not in a coercive way.

The biblical pronouncement about all creation is that "It is good, indeed, it is very good" (Genesis 1:31, NRSV). God's divine aim is to shape the world toward goodness and perfection. However, God's aim does not necessarily become the aim of human beings. Humans have the freedom to choose. And God's love aims, and love energies are focused on bringing about instrumental good. God seeks to lure humans toward this good. Yet because humans are self-actualizing persons, and have the freedom to choose, they must decide to accept God's good aim and so live as to make it become a reality. In this sense God's aim is soul making, making each of us the best possible person. This kind of soul making excludes the use of cruel accidents or forms of suffering. God does not coerce us, but allows us our freedom, all the while seeking to persuade and lure us toward goodness and love.

This understanding of God's power is in harmony with Jesus' life, teachings, and death, all of which show that Jesus chose persuasive love over coercive force. They also show God to be a God of persuasive love, not coercive power. Thus, the life and gentle teachings of Jesus are the touchstone of our faith. We must ever and again return to this life and teachings for understanding how to cope with evil in God's good creation.

The church must always be free to refresh its doctrines when they become stale stumbling blocks to unity and cooperative ministries in combating the evil in the world in Jesus' name. The church should also be flexible enough to allow for differing expressions of faith and doctrine in different religious bodies. Our pluralistic age in America and our world includes millions of people with differing expressions of faith and doctrine. Christianity is the largest religion with 2.22 billion followers. Islam is now the second largest religion in the world with 1.605 billion members, is rapidly growing, and may soon be larger than Christianity. Hinduism is the third largest religion with over 1.05 billion followers. Buddhism is the fourth largest religion in the world with over 488 million followers (All the numbers are from 2017 data). Such diversity requires that we seek a theology that is inclusive enough to allow for these other expressions of faith.

The most serious threat of the 21st century is that religious groups will set faith systems against one another. This danger is most evident with regard to Islam and Christianity. The toppling of the Twin Towers in New York City and the ensuing wars in Iraq and Afghanistan have created what many call a "cultural war" between

Islam and Christianity. The withdrawal of American troops from these war zones will not stop the clash of these two religions.

God, as **creative-responsive-kindness**, is confronting our war-torn world with unrealized aims and new possibilities at all times. These possibilities imply our need to seek a creative transformation of the present and to have an openness to the future. The literalist, whether fundamentalist or conservative, Muslim or Christian, will ultimately fail if this necessity for creative transformation is not realized and even encouraged, for rigidity fights against the essence of an everchanging universe.

To this point we have anchored evil in the creative process and attempted to understand God as creative-responsive kindness, rather than coercive force. We move forward on that basis to consider how to cope with evil.

Chapter Six

Christian Guidelines for Coping with Evil

Some of our greatest leaders have acknowledged the role of their mother in their lives. George Washington said,

> The greatest teacher I ever had was my mother.

Abraham Lincoln wrote,

> all that I am and
>
> all that I hoped to be, I
>
> owe my mother.

My parents wrote,

> love words in my heart
>
> that a cruel world can't erase.
>
> They never fail me.

I have learned some important lessons from observing Christian parents in the churches where I have been privileged to serve as minister. I also have had many parents say to me, "Give us some help in raising our families!" No one doubts the central and important role of parenting in raising children who can cope with evil and not be broken by the process. How can we strengthen our families?

Here are some guidelines I have found helpful in living my life and raising our family.

The first guideline for a healthy family

with strength to cope with evil is this:

Receive life as a precious gift from God.

In the church we hold our babies close, see the sparkle in their eyes, sense the mystery of life, and thank God as the giver of life. We see life as a gift and nurture life as a sacred responsibility. In Christian community we receive life and become life-givers.

Mothers and fathers are co-creators with God. As such their bodies are sacred temples. Good health practices are essential prior to conception and all through the period of gestation. Even during pregnancy stroking while using soothing words and music is helpful. This process of nurturing continues after birth and never ceases as long as the parents and the child live.

Many Christian churches celebrate the birth of a child with a prayer of dedication and some, as in my tradition, with infant baptism. Recognizing the sacredness of this event I often spoke these words at times of infant baptism:

O, Little One O, helpless one,

O, great receiver teach us.

Teach us

to be at home with gift,

to be at peace with need,

to rejoice in our belonging.

> Teach us
>
> to trust beyond all seeing,
>
> to be blessed beyond all knowing,
>
> to rest in God's pure being.
>
> (Adapted from Gerhard Frost, "To a Child,"
> *Homing in the Presence*, p. 75)

In infant baptism the church celebrates the child as a part of the covenant community, and the baptismal formula shows the child is enfolded in a relational trinity of kindness:

I baptize you in the name of the Father pictures God as becoming like a loving parent to the child. There is no greater human experience than the transforming power of love. The child belongs to God and is a child of God. God loves and cares for the child. God has called forth out of chaos a good and beautiful world, nurturing it through eons of time, for all of God's children to enjoy. All the children of God can actualize this goodness and beauty in their own lives.

I baptize you in the name of the Son. The life, death, and resurrection of Jesus are events at the heart of the New Testament gospel and reveal the unmerited and unconditional gracious love of God. God came in Jesus to fulfill covenant love and nurture novel love aims and purposes for children, and indeed for all people of the covenant. In his gentle life and tender teachings Jesus lived out these aims and purposes. As we hear the Gospel stories and learn more about Jesus, we can actualize these love aims and purposes in our lives. In this sense Jesus is the model for all humanity, without excluding other religious leaders who live and teach love, like Buddha who often said that the summary of my teaching is love.

I baptize you in the name of the Holy Spirit. In this new life God does not leave the child alone in confronting the world. God is present in Spirit to empower all God's children so they can live in ways that exhibit goodness and kindness and to encourage all of them in spiritual growth. Since we are self-actualizing persons, we have the potential to actualize, i.e. to do evil. The world has within it much evil to tempt us. But we believe God is constantly and, in every way, working to bring about good for all. God is persuasive rather than coercive; luring rather than forcing us to obey God's will.

God's power is shown in patience and love, not in force. This idea is at least as old as Plato and shaped the best characteristics of ancient Greek culture, including the virtues of beauty, goodness, and peace.

Therefore, God will be with all God's children at all times. God has promised never to leave us nor forsake us.

The baptism of children means that they have the covenant community of faith to help and encourage them, giving strength to cope with evil in a positive way. The church becomes God's hands doing God's work today when it practices tender teachings. The church is God's extended family and community where love and trust continue to grow. The church's power to influence is greater than the individual. In the church our children, youth, and adults hear the voice of God in sacred Scriptures, sermons, songs, and prayers.

The church is a community where visions are shaped and become like guiding lights for our daily living. These visions are inclusive, seeing each person as precious to us because they are precious in God's sight. These visions are of our family of faith living lives filled with God's loving aims and purposes, achieving truth, beauty, goodness, faith, hope, and love. And this is the adventure of a life-time of growth in kindness.

When our grandson was born to our daughter and son-in-law, our daughter was in her last year of medical school, and she needed help in caring for him so she could finish her schooling. As Beth and I were driving to Denver so we could provide some help Beth told me

>Just when I thought our
>
>parenting was all over,
>
>we are grandparents!

Our family was growing, and we wanted to continue to give guidance. Many children are growing up without family nurturing. A minister was visiting in a home one day and a little boy came to the door.

>The minister asked,
>
>Son is your father home?
>
>No, the little boy replied, He is out playing golf.
>
>Well, is your mother home?
>
>No, she is shopping.
>
>What about your older sister, is she home?
>
>No, she has gone to the movies with some friends.
>
>Then the minister said,
>
>Well, son, tell me.

> What are you doing here all by yourself?
>
> To which the lad replied,
>
> Oh, I wouldn't be here but
>
> I have our old white tom cat in the freezer
>
> trying to make a polar bear out of him.

Well, families are pulled in all directions today. Thus families need to find ways to transcend the noise of our time and recover togetherness.

We have a generation of youth who do not understand life is a precious gift. The violence in our society has robbed many of that sacred understanding. For some, life has become cheap and can be snuffed out like a video character on the computer screen.

Life is a gift from God, and it is to be received and nurtured as such all the days of our lives. This guideline is the starting point in developing a healthy relationship with God and in learning to cope with evil.

The second guideline for coping with evil is

to study the Bible and

seek to follow its teachings.

I grew up hearing my mother and grandmother read the Bible, and more importantly, feeling their kindness. My parents took me to church where I had my life peopled with prophets and saints. I heard dedicated Christians teaching the Bible and preachers boldly proclaiming the sacred Word.

The Psalmist wrote words that are special for this second guideline:

"Be to me a rock of refuge, a strong fortress,

to save me, for you are my rock and my fortress.

Rescue me, O my God, from the hand of the wicked,

from the grasp of the unjust and cruel.

For you, O Lord, are my hope,

my trust, O Lord, from my youth.

Upon you I have leaned from my birth;

it was you who took me from my mother's womb.

My praise is continually of you" (Psalm 71:3-6).

This Psalm gives a perfect example of how to commit our lives in trust to God from the womb to the tomb.

The apostle Paul said, "Fill your minds with those things that are good and that deserve praise; things that are true, noble, right, pure, lovely, and honorable. Put these things into practice and God will give you peace" (Philippians 4:8-9).

Society often models anger, hurt, and revenge. Young people can spend hours and hours on the World Wide Web and find information there on such ominous topics as "How to Build Bombs" that destroy and kill the most people. If we do not teach our young people about Bible study and prayer in our homes and churches, we are failing. In this New Testament passage we learn what is true, noble, right, pure, lovely, and honorable.

Erik Erikson, a noted developmental psychologist, studied in great depth the issue of trust/mistrust in a young child. He found that trust/mistrust is learned in the first two years of a child's life. The tender touching and nurturing of a child in these two years lays the foundation for a life of trust. Abuse leads to a life of mistrust.

As children are nurtured with tender care, they come to see their parent's trust and faith as trust in a loving God. Hosea gave us a picture of God that embodies this tender loving care. "When Israel was a child, I loved him. . . . I was the one who taught Israel to walk. I took my people up in my arms, I took care of them. I drew them to me in affection and love. I picked them up and held them to my cheek; I bent down to them and fed them" (Hosea 11). Hosea must have been nurtured by loving parents and the extended Jewish community for him to be able to give such a marvelous picture of God's wonderful love.

I was told of a marvelous experience of Christian nurturing between a mother and her daughter. Jen and Chuck Newell's five-year-old daughter, Ellie, was having difficulty sleeping one night. She said her pillow was too hard. Chuck switched beds with Ellie, so she could be with her mother for a while. Ellie's comment about her pillow caused Jen to think about Jacob sleeping in the wilderness with a rock for a pillow. This story seemed relevant, so Jen told her daughter. Each time Jen would finish a portion of the story, Ellie would ask, "Then what happened? Then Jen also told her other Bible stories about Jacob from his stealing Esau's blessing to that of his son, Joseph, rescuing his family from famine.

Since she had used the word *faith,* Jen decided to try to explain the meaning of faith. She said, "To have faith is to believe in God and trust God to take care of you." Ellie replied, "Oh, yes, and you know who really had faith? Moses' mother! To put her baby in a basket in the river, she had to have faith that God would take care of her baby." Then Ellie said, "I have lots of faith, from my head to the tips of my toes!" At that point Jen was overwhelmed with love. She told Ellie about how Jesus loved little children and about how children have the kind of faith Jesus wants all of us to have.

Nurturing children in faith and love is essential in their learning to cope with evil as they go out into the world with responsibility for making wise decisions.

The third guideline gives help for making wise decisions in times of temptations.

In my own times of temptations, I have found these questions to be helpful. (1). **Will the action I am contemplating harm my body**? This question is especially helpful if alcohol or drugs are concerned. My best friend would not have been killed in a cruel car accident when he was a senior in high school if he and his older brother had not been drinking and driving. If they had asked themselves this question: "Will this action harm my body?" everything could have been different. Remember that life is a precious gift! Harming one's body is degrading this precious gift. Mothers have organized and are making a difference in people's lives in the organization, MADD, Mothers Against Drunk Driving.

(2). Another question that has helped me is this: "**Will this action hurt the people I love and who love me**?" Will my mother, my father, my family be sad? I had a church member who became enmeshed in unethical business practices. The evil was woven one strand at a time much like a spider weaves a web. Then one day the man found he was trapped, snared in the web of deceit. He became the fall guy for company policies that were much bigger than he. He went to prison for a while.

Many were the days when asking this question would have helped him: "Will my decisions and actions hurt my family, the people I love and who love me?" Of course, he and his family were devastated. Merely asking this question, "Will my actions hurt my family?" can turn our thoughts to the people who love us and can turn us away from actions that will hurt them.

3). A third question has helped me: "**Will God be pleased or disappointed by this action I am contemplating**?" In the Gospel of John, we find this promise: Those who love me will keep my word, and my Father will love them, and we will come to them and make our home with them" (John 14:23, NRSV). This is not a promise to visit from time to time. It is a promise to come and make a home with us permanently. Like a loving parent, God moves in with us and cares for us. Like a child confidently talks with a parent, we can talk with God and listen to God's still small voice that is within us. With this kind of intimacy our question takes on real meaning: "Will my thoughts and actions hurt and make God sad?" Merely asking this question can turn us toward actions that are just, pure, and noble.

As we view the radical evil in our world today, we ask, "What went wrong?" The problem is complicated. There is no easy answer. But I believe these Christian guidelines will be helpful, and nurturing parents and caregivers can lead the way as they often do.

In *The Presbyterian Outlook*, Edmond McDonald writes about the transforming power of this nurturing love:

When God wants an important thing done in this world or a wrong righted, this is how God goes about it.

God doesn't release

Thunder bolts or stir up earthquakes.

God simply has a tiny baby born,

> perhaps of a very humble mother.
>
> And God puts the idea or purpose into the mother's heart.
>
> And she puts it in the baby's mind; and then, God waits—
>
> Expecting goodwill to become incarnate in each human life.
>
> (Quoted in *Guide My Feet*, Marion Wright Edelman, p. 7)

The Church must also be in the forefront, nurturing the gift of life. Virginia Satir in *People Making* says that many adults have never known what it feels like to be accepted and enjoyed by another person. There is no acceptance like the acceptance into the family of God. As we gather before an open Bible in worship our lives are enlarged and "peopled" by prophets and apostles who come alive and challenge us. We learn that Jesus is our friend. As our lives are peopled with the "Savior and saints" we gain dreaming capacities for great adventures in the kingdom of God.

In these quiet times of prayer and worship we gain a deep sense of peace. In a world of rapid change all of us need this gift of peace and security—a feeling that we belong. Linus and his security blanket in the comic strip, Peanuts, are the perfect image of this need in the lives of children and youth. In writing to young Timothy, Paul spoke of his security as grounded in faith in God:

> I know whom I have believed
>
> and I am convinced that God is able to guard
>
> what I have been entrusted with (2 Timothy 1:12).

Paul wanted Timothy to have the same sense of security—being guarded by God's powerful Spirit.

Before Jesus left this world for the next, he promised to send his followers a helper who would hold them in security and peace. I will never forget how one minister expressed the way his father and mother communicated a feeling of security to him that was life-long.

He said that when he was a small boy his father traveled a lot. On the nights his father was returning home, his mother usually let him stay up a little later to see his father. However, on this particular day he had been disobedient, and his mother sent him to bed early. When he heard his father's voice in the lower hallway, he jumped out of bed, hesitated for a moment wondering if he would be reprimanded. However, out of a desire to see his father, he ran on down the stairs.

At the foot of the stairs his father met him, swept him up into his arms, held him close and with his mother joining the family hug, and said,

> "Our son, our son, how
>
> we love you."

Then hearing of his disobedience, he sent him back upstairs to bed. But it did not matter, for the love and acceptance of his family voiced by his father and made real in the family hug, gave him a security that never left him.

Parents are the guardians of a healthy family. Would you like for your family to be strengthened? Learn how to cope with evil and not be broken by evil. Then take time to worship and to sit quietly and talk about family needs. And may God keep all our families in faith with its gift of peace, grounded in goodness, grace, and love

Chapter Seven

A New Kindness

My Apple I-phone app shows that I walked 2085 miles in the last twelve months. As I walked, I often contemplated this book on God and evil, asking— What is the meaning of life? How does one balance good and evil? As I walked, I closely, silently observed God's

Miracle of Love

Every snow flake different,

the snowshoe hare with puff tail

hopping across the powdery trail,

the eagle tipping his white cap,

the ptarmigan with white winter plumage,

sweeping the snow from spruce limbs

with feathery broom.

What is the meaning of life filled with good and evil?

One blessed person's lifetime bio—

Of joy and delight

a miracle of love

a new kindness

for coping with evil

Observing poetry in nature

is teaching me to contemplate,

be still, and pay attention to

the p's and q's on the plate,

moving from the big picture

to the smallest detail,

and then looking back at the big scene

with new meaning.

In these contemplative moments, I find God's notebook open, revealing secret wonders, mysterious answers. As I walk silently contemplating,

I observe a moose in the wild

Gazing upon its garden-of-Eden-like home.

Feet caressing the grassy carpet of the floors.

Eyes surveying the snowcapped mountains of its walls,

ears pointing to the glass dome of its roof.

Still, quiet, contemplating,

praying with focused mind.

If this is not Eden,

If this is not prayer,

I don't know what is!

Be still, my soul.

Have faith!

Goodness is everywhere!

At a time when many are abandoning the church and ordinary words are no longer sufficient to communicate the extraordinary, perhaps it is time to return to the beauty of nature for inspiration and hope; and let the birds and flowers speak to us and sing the music of the soul. As long as nature speaks, I will listen and pray. Each time I go gently into nature with the music of my soul almost gone, I return with a symphony.

Blessed by Nature---

I have sipped nectar

from the cup of wildflowers on our Alaska farm.

I have seen a snowshoe hare dancing with white stocking feet.

I have measured my hand

Against a bear's paw print.

I have gazed from our tree house as a mother moose

licked her new born twins.

I have watched an alpenglow sunrise

and been blessed by the beauty of nature.

Wisdom comes in taking the gifts given each day

and enjoying them to the fullest.

As I start walking, I am painfully aware of the brokenness of our divided world photographed and viewed on TV as violence and destruction. Evil is as old as that scaly old serpent in the garden of Eden in the biblical story. As I walk and let nature sing its healing song to me, I am shedding my scaly snake skin stained by prejudice, in order to grow a new skin, one shining with love and kindness, shaped by the gentle life and tender teachings of Jesus. **And this may be the best defense against evil that is available to us.**

Kindness is like a beautiful stained-glass window that gathers the light of heaven and warms all in its glow.

Kindness is the most healing force in the world. Nature holds the cup of kindness for all of us to drink. In drinking the cup of kindness, we gain our greatest defense against evil and transforming the evils of society.

Go gently into nature and

drink deeply.

Chapter Eight

A Relational Hermeneutic of Kindness for Interpreting the Bible's Story

"One touch of nature makes the whole world kin." William Shakespeare

"I am God. I am merciful and kind" (Based on Exodus 33:19, CEV).

"Our Lord, you bless those who live right, and you shield them with your kindness" (Psalm 5:11, CEV).

Jesus described his ministry in these words: "If you are tired from carrying heavy burdens, come to me and I will give you rest. . . Learn from me. I am gentle and humble, and you will find rest" (Matthew 11:28-29, CEV).

"God our Savior showed us goodness and kindness." (Titus 3:4, CEV).

This chapter seeks to develop a relational hermeneutic of kindness for interpreting the Bible and showing its relevance to life (For a fuller treatment of my hermeneutic of kindness see my book, *A Relational Hermeneutic of Kindness*). Hermeneutics is defined in the broad sense as the science of reflecting on how words and events of the past may become meaningful in the present.

Traditionally, biblical hermeneutics has sought to answer two questions: What did the biblical text mean when it was written? And what does the text mean today?

For many the first question answers the second. What it meant when it was written is a timeless and eternal truth, and that is the meaning today. However, hermeneutics acknowledges a gap between the centuries that is not so easily spanned. For example, take the verse, "When God's people meet in church, the women must not be allowed to speak. They must keep quiet and listen, as the law of Moses teaches. If there is something they want to know, they can ask their husbands when they get home. It is disgraceful for women to speak in church" (1 Corinthians 14:33b-35 CEV).

The people of God have had difficulty in interpreting texts like this one that clearly reflect cultural traditions and not timeless truths. Without going into the lengthy process of answering the two questions posed above, this chapter seeks to offer a unifying hermeneutical concept that can help us deal with difficult biblical texts.

A Relational Hermeneutic of Kindness

Relational Kindness is a good hermeneutic for interpreting the Bible. I am proposing a relational **trinity** of kindness:

I believe God is kind.

I believe Jesus is kind and calls us to be kind.

I believe Spirit is Jesus alive in the Church teaching kindness.

In general, I am using kindness as a unifying biblical concept that seeks to elucidate the relational nature of reality, **emphasizing becoming rather than static existence of all things.** The Bible is about relationships from Genesis to Revelation where everything is continually changing with the evolutionary energy of kindness. In the first book of the Bible we have a beautiful mythic-poetic account of God walking in the new Garden of Eden with Adam and Eve and in the last book of the Bible the old earth and the old heaven are passing away and the new earth and new heaven are continually being born.

The old is not an enduring unchanging substance; it is continually experienced as new events. The mythic Poetry of Genesis is well suited to express evolving life

within the sphere of good and evil.

>Looking at what was evolving

>out of chaos

>God pronounced

>that it was good

>adding for emphasis,

>it is very good.

>The snake is there

>with a mischievous grin!

As the story of good and evil unfolds in human history, a hermeneutic is essential to unravel the mystery. For me, the theme of kindness is the best lens through which to understand this mystery and learn how to cope with evil:

>The gentle teachings of the biblical writers

>slowly but surely change our lives and our world.

Gentle teachings are especially suited as a hermeneutic, a prism through which we view and interpret the Bible. God's kindness transforms life. This is my hermeneutic from Alpha to Omega, from beginning to end. The kindness of God shines throughout the Bible. And that kindness has transforming energy. Here is the heartbeat of my hermeneutic:

> The kindness we show to ourselves, our family,
>
> and to all living things
>
> is the greatest healing force in the world.

Relational Kindness and Covenant

My hermeneutic of kindness is a summation of a thousand years of God's covenantal loving kindness revealed in the Old Testament, and in the tender teachings of Jesus in the New Testament.

> The biblical image of faith is
>
> a child wrapped in the folds of a mother's garments
>
> where there is security,
>
> nurturing,
>
> love,
>
> and kindness.

Psalm 22:9-10 expresses the theme of God's kindness, a note that is beautifully sounded often in the Psalms:

> "God, you brought me safely through birth,
>
> and you protected me as a baby at my mother's breast.

> From the day that I was born
>
> I have been in your tender care,
>
> and from my birth you have been by my side."

The faith stories of the prophets and poets of Israel that tell of God's tender care are Jesus' religious past and they are creatively brought together through a process of selective prehension, feeling each one personally, to become Jesus' new gentle teachings.

The reality of the transforming power of kindness is conceived as a process of creative advance in which many past faith events are integrated in the events of Jesus' present healing ministry, and in turn are taken up by future events.

The universe creatively advances as a sequence of integrations of these tender teachings at every level and moment of existence. This creative advance is especially seen in Revelation where the risen Jesus is alive in the church, his new body, where his kindness continues to transform suffering (See, *The Book of Revelation: Jesus' Kindness Transforms Suffering* for this understanding of Revelation).

Relational Kindness is Unifying

John's vision of heaven in Revelation lifts everything from earth to heaven, starting with the crucified Jesus, the Lamb that was slain. The suffering of Jesus is brought before the throne of God and absorbed in creative responsive love. In this divine action union with God as One is completed and transformed into heavenly reality as the risen Jesus passes back into the world as a new creation.

The risen Jesus gathers a community, as a mother hen gathers her chicks. In this community the risen Jesus lives and continues his ministry empowered by God's Spirit, the same Spirit that empowered the prophets, Jesus' historical ministry, and spiritual leaders in other faith traditions.

The hermeneutic of kindness is about this Spirit of inclusion that joins all love energies into one redemptive healing force that has the power to change our lives and our world.

Relational Kindness and Ministry

Kindness is not only a unifying concept that holds the biblical message together, kindness also transcends the gap between the biblical world and today. Relational kindness makes the biblical message relevant today.

> As we send kindness into the world
>
> with wings,
>
> walls of prejudice fall down,
>
> sexual barriers are transcended,
>
> including persons of differing sexual preferences,
>
> anger and hatred are healed,
>
> poisoned water is made clean,
>
> and hungry children are fed.

This transformative action of relational kindness in the world also transforms God, for kindness is reciprocal in nature.

What is done in the world is lifted to heaven where all things become new and pass back into the world making all things new.

This is God's love for the world.

God's kingdom is now present on earth as it is in heaven.

God is now

in the world in new ways

and for the world

in new tidal waves of saving loving kindness.

Alfred North Whitehead, the father of process philosophy, affirmed that the temporal process is a momentary transition from one actual entity to another. These entities are themselves momentary events which perish immediately upon coming into being. The perishing marks the transition to the succeeding events. We see this in the Bible in covenant love between God and the people of God where the old is passing away and the new is being born. Time is not a single smooth flow but comes into being as a series of events: the old covenant with Moses and prophets and the new covenant with Jesus and each succeeding generation in all faith traditions.

When Christians affirm that Jesus is the fulfillment of the old covenant this is not a negation of the old or the only way the newness is expressed. Faith progresses in many religious traditions from the past, into the present, and into the future, always in mysterious and new ways. Every moment of transformative kindness is new and provides the datum for new processes to happen as creative advancement.

Relational Kindness is Persuasive and Luring

A relational hermeneutic of kindness seeks to understand God and how God relates to the world from this metaphysical perspective of experiential events rather than enduring substances. This is in contrast to much traditional theology that is based on a mechanistic model that sees the world as made up of unchanging building blocks that bounce like billiard balls when hit by the cue stick. Protons and atoms bounce off each other unaffected in this static view, giving a view of cosmic and biological evolution as re-arrangement of the building blocks.

Using kindness as a relational hermeneutic says that in the course of evolution change occurs in subjects, not objects. In traditional theology based on understanding the universe as a mechanistic universe of unchanging objects, God manipulates and causes all things that happen; even accidents and natural disasters are interpreted from this perspective. The Bible portrays the shadow side of human nature and since this human earthly nature is always connected on another level to the divine heavenly nature, we should not try to separate the two levels in the Bible. Kindness unifies these experiences.

This fits the Relational hermeneutic of kindness that sees all things inter-connected and inter-related, seeing

God in the world

and for the world,

in us

and for us

acting in kind saving ways.

Relational kindness allows for individual freedom in the evolutionary process and sees individual self-determination and self-actualization as key to understanding human existence. In the story of the Bible,

> God understands and cares for
>
> the ones who are suffering.
>
> God is in the relational process setting
>
> novel aims and purposes,
>
> luring the struggling people of God in the fulfillment of
>
> these aims and purposes
>
> that are always good and loving.

Kindness reveals that God is not coercive in this relationship but persuasive and luring. God relates to the world from within as gentle persuasive activity. In Revelation, the last book of the Bible, we see this divine activity as the Spirit of God and the Spirit of the risen Jesus directing the new community in transforming ways.

To be sure John, like some Old Testament writers, does not always see this activity through the eyes of Kindness, and we must respect his freedom in seeing things from his world view. At times he is almost totally consumed by suffering.

Yet, his use of creative images allows us to pick them up and interpret them through the lens of kindness that he sets before us in the introduction to Revelation in these words:

> "I pray that you will be blessed with kindness
>
> and peace from God,
>
> who is and was and is coming" (1:4, CEV).

To make sure we do not miss his concern for kindness, John closes his book with this prayer:

"I pray . . . Jesus will be kind to all of you" (22:21, CEV).

John's lens of kindness invites us to flesh out his images of suffering, wrath, and vengeance with the kindness of God revealed in the tender teachings of the biblical writers; and especially for us, in the gentle life and tender teachings of Jesus we have in the four Gospels and the entire New Testament.

A hermeneutic of kindness allows us to interpret the biblical message in transforming ways, especially the difficult passages that seem to sanction wars of violence and aggression. And this is my hermeneutic for interpreting the whole Bible from Genesis to Revelation. I have especially found this hermeneutic of kindness helpful in understanding God and evil.

Relational Kindness and World View

Whereas traditional theology saw God as passionless, as a perfect unchanging being, the hermeneutical task requires that we translate the message of God through our scientific world view. As Christians we affirm that God is the source of all truth. Integrity requires that we incorporate scientific truth with our belief in God as the source of truth.

Israel's faith stories lend themselves well to being interpreted through a relational hermeneutic of kindness that is balanced with scientific truth. Using relational kindness as my interpretive lens, enables me to say that God feels the feelings of all creation as responsive beneficiary, not benefactor only. A relational hermeneutic of kindness emphasizes the immanence of God, seeing God as synthesis of all our feelings and all feelings of the universe, and God is changed by this concrescence, this reciprocal activity of becoming through the unification of many feelings in which the many become one.

In biblical terms this is God loving the world and saving the world (see John 3:16, For God so loved the world). Concrescence in reference to persons is the act of becoming by unifying the possibilities presented by God's loving action in the world and for the world, in us and for us. Humans are partially created by their heredity and environment, what is given to them from the past, the present, and the lure of God; but humans exercise personal choice in the continuing process of becoming. Psychologically speaking, this is self-actualization.

Nurturing love is reciprocal in nature. God both gives and receives kindness and reciprocal kindness changes all coming into its warmth and glow. One touch of kindness makes us all kin.

In summary, the following are key concepts in my relational hermeneutic of kindness used in understanding God and evil.

(1) Relational. The way entities are interconnected and have relevance to one another. In the biblical message God, Jesus, and Spirit are interrelated as One in the experience of loving kindness in a cosmic community of becoming.

(2) Immanence. God is in all things. This is not pantheism which says that all things are God. Relational hermeneutics stresses that God is in all things as immanence, but God transcends all things as well, having creative power of persuasion, distinct from the universe.

(3) A reciprocal relationship of kindness between God and the world. It is as true to say that God is present in the world meeting each entity with kindness as to say that the world is present in God experiencing tender saving care. One of the main contributions of a relational hermeneutic of kindness is the change from a subject-

object schema to subject-subject approach to interpretation. The biblical story as the revelation of God's kindness addresses the interpreter as subject. This reciprocal relationship of kindness transforms our lives, our ministry, and our world.

(4) Integrity of the natural order. For autonomous self-actualizing entities to emerge in the evolutionary ongoing process, it is necessary that the natural order be organized and regular, and therefore comprehensible to all evolving entities, including persons.

My hermeneutic of kindness adds to this "integrity of the natural order," insights from E. O. Wilson that humans have evolved with an innate need to relate to all of nature and to all other life forms. Two Greek words, βιος and φιλια are joined together to form "biophilia" and conveys love for all life forms. I have fleshed out Wilson's insightful and exciting theory of biophilia with the gentle teachings of the Bible.

(5) God as Spirit is the supremely related entity, One with the universe in creative responsive kindness.

(6) God's relational loving kindness is the guiding principle and ground of all ethical actions. In meeting each entity with kindness God gives intrinsic value that calls us to be kind to all other entities.

(7) Ecumenical Spirit: Kindness is a theme in most religions of the world. Buddha said often, "My teaching is kindness." For Christians Jesus is the best example of relational love, but this does not negate other religious leaders in all faith traditions. Also, Jesus' life and death, to have transforming power for us, must not violate the integrity of the natural order as defined in number four above. The miracle of the biblical stories is that they speak to people with all kinds of world views. I can sing hymns with bad theology and say the Apostles' Creed with its archaic language and do it as a sense of becoming one with the saints of the past and as a part of the

communities of faith today that often have diverse views of Scripture. I can do this and still interpret the images through the gentle teachings of Jesus for myself, personally without excluding others.

The kindness of God revealed in the biblical writers and the gentle teachings of Jesus form the core of my faith and become the lens through which I interpret the biblical message. The remaining question is this: Does the hermeneutic of kindness show us how our life experiences should be interpreted and written? I humbly and prayerfully suggest that it does. Living God's loving kindness is the best way for us to overcome the violence that threatens to destroy us.

In making relational kindness my hermeneutic for interpreting the Bible and our life experience; and in this book for understanding God and evil, some may feel that I am packing too much meaning in this one word, kindness. In my linguistic studies I have found that words do not have meaning, they have usage. Context determines how a word is used and what its meaning should be. For example, the word, bank, has many usages. If I say that I am taking a check to the bank, it has a clear meaning by the context in which I use it. If I say that he is fishing on the river bank, bank has a different meaning. If I say she made a perfect bank shot, bank has another usage and meaning.

My use of the word kindness broadens each time it is used to interpret the ways God relates to us in the biblical writers and in Jesus' gentle teaching and the ways we become kind in this adventurous journey into the mystery of God's relational ways. The adventure belongs to the adventurous, and I hope you will feel my excitement as you learn more about being kind to others.

A Relational hermeneutic of kindness also fits the needs of our global pluralistic age. Many religions including Judaism, Islam, and Buddhism stress the theme of kindness. Isaac Bashevis Singer, author and Nobel Prize in Literature winner (1978) wrote,

"Kindness, I've discovered, is everything in life."

Finally, this is my experience: God meets each occasion of my life with kindness and this inspires me to be kind to others, starting with my family and moving out in an ever-widening circle of kindness that is all-inclusive.

I may not be able to give all the kindness the world needs, but the world needs all the kindness I can give. In the end, then, kindness is victorious. (See my books, *A Relational Trinity of Kindness* and *A Center that Holds: Adventures in Kindness* for more biblical support for this Trinity of hermeneutical kindness).

Kindness Blessing

May kindness be in our thoughts,

making them good and loving.

May kindness be in our eyes,

leading us to see what is just in life.

May kindness be in our hands and feet

so that we may be of service to others.

May kindness be in our whole being –

Making us one with God and the universe.

I don't know how to define kindness,

but I know for sure when I feel it.

Religious Poetry and Hermeneutic

In seminary I studied

devotional classics.

Visited Thomas Merton

at Gethsemane Monastery

and saw the importance of a contemplative lifestyle.

Fifty years later

I still go quietly

into nature

as my hermitage

to meditate on reality.

Nature speaks to me

and UNLIKE much human activity

the message is

logical and coherent.

In nature all is integrally related.

This revelation is universally applicable to daily living.

Poetry exhibits this reality

of one in all

and all in one.

In my religious poetry

God is the One unifying actuality.

God evolves in relationship

with the evolving world.

Religion, science,

sociology, and psychology,

Indeed, all the ologies

are fused into poetic thought

with alpenglow-ology.

Alpenglow poetic imagination

gives birth to what is unrealized,

in human terms,

In the womb of nature.

Awake from sleep,

oh my soul.

Go out into God's universe---

Hear the call of nature.

See beauty.

Shake the world.

Conclusion

Writing about God and evil is a curious endeavor, swerving from puzzlement into delirium, and from madness into stretches of calm assurance. It is almost impossible for us two-legged animals, having evolved through unrecorded history to putting words and thoughts on pages and computer screens, to write about God and evil.

Our spoken words are borne by the same air that nourishes plants, flowers, birds, animals, giant spruce trees, and the orographic clouds written by the 250 mile Chugach Alaskan mountains range. Our words, whether we speak them or put them on a computer screen, represent the world around us just as the etchings of the first humans put on the walls of the caves in which they lived represent their thoughts and utterances. Our thoughts and words always reflect the world around us, i.e., our world view.

One's world view is especially important when discussing God and evil. For example, my thoughts on God and evil expressed in this book have been filtered through my 79 years of life on the planet earth and over 50 years of reading science, philosophy, world religions, psychology, and being exposed to vast arrays of art, literature, and music. As one who majored in New Testament Greek in my graduate studies and translated the four Gospels and most of the New Testament from Greek to English, I also understand God and evil through the prism of the gentle life and tender teachings of Jesus.

I speak *about* evil whereas primitive persons spoke *to* evil in the air, water, rocks, and animals; and these inanimate and animate things spoke back to them. Obviously, these things do not speak in human words. However, the birds speak their language as do all earthly things; and human language shares a dimension with all other things.

Each of us have our own personal world view that shapes how we see God and evil. As a husband, father, and grandfather I often ask, "Does my view of God and evil, my understanding of the world in which I live, help me to be a more gentle person in all of my personal relationships?" My answer is "Yes, I am happy and at peace." This is my prayer for you as you continue to explore these mysteries.

Be Kind

As a linguist,

I have seen how words are powerful

and the precursor to action---

Hostile words often lead

to hostile actions.

Kindness is like honey---

Sweet to the taste

and healing to the soul.

Taste and see that God is

good,

loving,

and kind.

Be kind to one another.

Part 2

As a poet,

how do you spend your day?   I am kind.

With Breaking News all day,

how do you focus?   I am kind.

In becoming the voice of the little ones, how do you remain sincere?   I am kind.

In an age of global disbelief, how do you center on God. I am kind.

Bibliography

Aslan, Reza. *Zealot*. New York: Random House. 2013

Aune, D. E. "The Apocalypse of John and Greco-Roman Revelatory Magic," *New Testament Studies*, 33. 1987.

_____. "The Form and Function of the Proclamation to the Seven Churches (Revelation 2-3)," *New Testament Studies*, 1990

Barr, D. L. "The Apocalypse as a Symbolic Transformation of the World: A Literary Analysis," *Interpretation*. 38 (1984), 39-50.

Bauckham, Richard. *The Theology of the Book of Revelation*. New Testament Theology. Cambridge: Cambridge University Press, 1993.

Beale, G. K. *The Book of Revelation: A Commentary on the Greek Text*. The New International Greek Testament Commentary. Grand Rapids: Eerdmans, 2013

Beasley-Murray, G. R. *The Book of Revelation*. New Century Bible. London: Marshal, Morgan & Scott, 1974.

Bernstein, Richard J. *Radical Evil: A Philosophical Interrogation*. Cambridge: Polity Press, 2002.

Boring, M. Eugene. *Revelation*. Interpretation. Louisville: John Knox, 1989.

Bracken, Joseph A. S.J. and Marjorie Hewitt Suchocki, ed. *Trinity in Process: A Relational Theology of God*. New York: Continuum Publishing Co., 1997.

Caird, G. B. *The Revelation of St. John the Divine*. Harper's New Testament Commentary. New York: Harper and Row. 1966.

Cobb, John B. Jr. *Becoming a Thinking Christian*. Nashville: Abingdon Press, 1993. _____. *Christ In A Pluralistic Age*. Eugene, Or: Wipf and Stock Publishers, 1998.

_____. *Lay Theology*. St. Louis: Chalice Press, 1994

Cole, Dwayne. *A Center that Holds: Adventures in Kindness*. Cleveland, Tennessee: Parson's Porch Books, 2015.

_____. *A Prayer of Blessing: As You Go Remember This*. Cleveland, Tennessee: Parson's Porch Books, 2015.

_____. *A Relational Trinity of Kindness*. Cleveland, Tennessee: Parson's Porch Books, 2015.

_____. *Jesus' Transforming Beatitudes: Selected Sermons from Year A*. Cleveland, Tennessee: Parson's Porch Books, 2015.

_____. *Jesus' Transforming Love: Selected Sermons from Year B*. Cleveland, Tennessee: Parson's Porch Books, 2014.

_____. *Jesus' Transforming Gentle Teachings: Selected Sermons from Year C. Cleveland, Tennessee: Parson' Porch Books, 2015*.

_____. *The Apostles' Creed: A Living Creed for the Living Church*. Cleveland, Tennessee: Parson's Porch Books, 2014

_____. *The Book of Revelation: Jesus' Kindness Transforms Suffering*. Cleveland, Tennessee: Parson's Porch Books, 2015.

_____. *The Serenity Prayer: A Pathway to Peace and Happiness*. Cleveland, Tennessee: Parson's Porch Books, 2015.

_____. *The Story of the Bible: Authority, Inspiration, Canonization, and Translation*. Cleveland, Tennessee: Parson's Porch Books, 2015.

_____. "Taking the Pulse of the Universe," *The Cumberland Presbyterian Magazine,* January 2004.

_____. "Jesus Prays for the Church: Sermon Preached to the General Assembly of the Cumberland Presbyterian Church," *The Cumberland Presbyterian Magazine,* 1998.

_____. "Baptism and the Lord's Supper in the Gospel of John: A Hermeneutical Enquiry." A Ph. D. dissertation at The Southern Baptist Theological Seminary, Louisville, Ky. 1973.

Daley, B. *The Hope of the Early Church.* Cambridge: Cambridge University Press, 1991.

Davis, Stephen T. Editor. *Encountering Evil: Live Options in Theodicy.* Atlanta: John Knox Press, 1981.

deSilva, David A. *Introducing the Apocalypse: Message, Context, and Significance.* Grand Rapids: Baker Academic. 2002.

Eagleton, Terry. *On Evil.* New Haven: Yale University Press, 2010.

Edwards, George R. *Jesus and the Politics of Violence.* New York: Harper & Row, 1972.

Ehrman, Bart D. *How Jesus Became God.* New York: Harper Collins Publishers, 2014.

Feuillet, A. *The Apocalypse.* Trans. T. E. Crane. New York: Alba House, 1965.

Ford, Lewis S. *The Lure of God: A Biblical Background for Process Theism.* Philadelphia: Fortress Press. 1978.

_____. *Transforming Process Theism.* Albany: State University Press. 2000.

Frank, Viktor E. Man's *Search for Meaning: An Introduction to Logotherapy*. Third Edition. New York: Simon & Schuster, 1984.

_____. The Will to Meaning: Foundations and Applications of Logotherapy. Expanded Edition. New York: Meridian, 1988

Gregg, Steve. *Revelation: Four Views*. Revised and Updated. Nashville: Thomas Nelson, 2011.

Griffin, David R. God, Power, and Evil: A Process Theodicy. Philadelphia: The Westminster Press, 1976.

_____and John B. Cobb. *Process Theology: An Introductory Exposition*. Philadelphia: The Westminster Press, 1976.

Hartshorne, Charles. *The Divine Relativity*. New Haven: Yale University Press, 1948.

Hicks, John H. *Evil and the God of Love*. New York: Harper & Row, 1977.

Jung, C. G. *Archetypes and the Collective Unconscious*. B. F. C. Hull, translator. Bollingen Series XX. Princeton University Press, 1969.

_____. *Encountering Jung: On Evil*. Selected and Introduced by Murray Stein. Princeton: Princeton University Press. 1995.

Karr-Morse. Robin and Meredith S. Wiley, *Ghosts from the Nursery: Tracing the Roots of Violence*. New York: The Atlantic Monthly Press, 1997.

Kasemann, Ernst. *Jesus Means Freedom*. Translated by Frank Clarke. Philadelphia: Fortress Press, 1971.

Keller, Catherine. *On the Mystery: Discerning Divinity in Process*. Minneapolis Fortress Press, 2008.

Kidwell, Clara Sue, Homer Noley, and George E. "Tink" Tinker. *A Native American Theology*. New York: Orbis Books, 2001.

McFague, Sallie. *Models of God*. Minneapolis: Augsburg Fortress, 1987.

_____. *The Body of God: An Ecological Theology*. Minneapolis: Augsburg Fortress, 1993.

Medved, Michael and Diane Medved. *Saving Childhood: Protecting Our Children from the National Assault on Innocence*. New York: Harper Colins Publishers, 1998.

Murphy, R. "An Allusion to Mary in the Apocalypse," *Theological Studies*, 2:565-73, 1949.

Neiman, Susan. *Evil in Modern Thought: An Alternative History of Philosophy*. Princeton: Princeton University Press, 2002.

Pagels, Elaine. *Revelations: Visions, Prophecy, & Politics in the Book of Revelation*. New York: Penguin Group. 2012.

_____. *The Origin of Satan*. New York: Random House, 1995.

Parkin, David. *The Anthropology of Evil*. New York: Basil Blackwell, Inc., 1985.

Peterson, Michael L. Editor. The Problem of Evil: Selected Readings. Notre Dame, Indiana: University of Notre Dame Press, 1992.

Robben, Antonius C. G. M. and Marcelo M. Suarez-Orozco, eds. *Cultures under Seige: Collective Violence and Trauma*. Cambridge: Cambridge University Press, 2000.

Rowland, Christopher C. "The Book of Revelation." *The New Interpreter's Bible*, Vol. XII, Abingdon Press, 1998

Salzberg, S. *Lovingkindness: The Revolutionary Art of Happiness*. Boston: Shambhala, 2002.

Schmithals, Walter. *The Apocalyptic Movement*. John E. Steely, editor. Nashville: Abingdon Press, 1975.

Snider, Tim. *All Things New: Understanding the Book of Revelation*. Bloomington: WestBow Press, 2011.

Suchocki, Marjorie Hewitt. *God Christ Church: A Practical Guide to Process Theology*. New Revised Edition. New York: The Crossroad Publishing Company, 1989.

_____. *The End of Evil: Process Eschatology in Historical Context*. Albany: State University, 1988.

_____. *In God's Presence: Theological Reflections on Prayer*. St. Louis: Chalice Press, 1996.

The Greek New Testament, Ed. Kurt Aland, Matthew Black, Carlo M. Martini, Bruce Metzger, and Allen Wikgren. Third Edition. United Bible Societies, 1975.

Thompson, Leonard L. *The Book of Revelation: Apocalypse and Empire*. New York: Oxford University Press. 1990.

Tobin, Thomas. "Logos," *The Anchor Bible Dictionary*, Vol. 4. New York: Doubleday, 1992.

Tournier, Paul. *The Violence Within*. Trans. Edwin Hudson. San Francisco: Harper & Row, 1978.

Wainwright, A. *Mysterious Apocalypse*. Nashville: Abingdon, 1993.

Whitehead, Alfred North. *Adventures of Ideas*. New York: The Free Press, 1967.

_____. *Process and Reality*. Corrected Edition, ed. David Ray Griffin and Donald W. Sherburne. New York: The Free Press, 1978.

_____. *Modes of Thought*. New York: The Free Press, 1968.

Wink, Walter. *Engaging the Powers: Discernment and Resistance in a World of Domination*. Minneapolis: Fortress Press, 1992.

_____. *Naming the Powers: The Language of Power in the New Testament*. Philadelphia: Fortress Press, 1984

_____. *Unmasking the Powers: The Invisible Forces that Determine Human Existence*. Philadelphia: Fortress Press, 1986

Woodruff, Paul and Harry A. Wilmer, Editors. *Facing Evil: Light at the Core of Darkness*. Lasalle, Illinois: Open Court Publishing Company, 1988.

Other Books by Dwayne Cole

A Center that Holds: Adventures in Kindness.

A Prayer of Blessing: As You Go Remember This.

A Relational Hermeneutic of Kindness.

A Relational Trinity of Kindness.

God and Evil: An Ode to Kindness.

Jesus' Transforming Beatitudes: Selected Sermons from Year A.

Jesus' Transforming Love: Selected Sermons from Year B.

Jesus' Transforming Gentle Teachings: Selected Sermons from Year C.

The Apostles' Creed: A Living Creed for the Living Church.

The Book of Revelation: Jesus' Kindness Transforms Suffering.

The Serenity Prayer: A Pathway to Peace and Happiness.

The Story of the Bible: Authority, Inspiration, Canonization, and Translation.

www.ingramcontent.com/pod-product-compliance
Lightning Source LLC
Chambersburg PA
CBHW052200110526
44591CB00012B/2020